PRAISE FOR JOHN COUSINS

You are motivating many! You are inspiring many! You are adding great value to many!

— Nicole Chin

I am a big fan of your books, which make all these difficult topics really easy to understand. This is excellent work.

— Adnan

I just finished your MBA ASAP Corporate Finance Fundamentals on Udemy! It was fantastic! I learned so much. Thank you

— Cherryl

I have no words to describe your writing except that you left me with an Oh moment.

— Haneen

PREVENT PISS POOR PERFORMANCE WITH PLANNING

MBA ASAP STRATEGIC PLAN TEMPLATE

JOHN COUSINS

First published by BizB Press 2019

Copyright © 2019 by John J. Cousins

BizB supports copyright. Copyright fuels creativity, encourages diverse voices, promotes free speech, and creates vibrant culture. Thank you for buying an authorized edition of this book and for complying with copyright laws by not reproducing, scanning, or distributing any part of it in any form without permission. You are supporting writers and allowing BizB to continue to publish books for every reader.

ISBN: 9798551720263

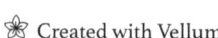 Created with Vellum

"To think is easy. To act is hard. But the hardest thing in the world is to act in accordance with your thinking."

— Johann Wolfgang von Goethe

A goal properly set is halfway reached.

— Zig Ziglar

PREFACE

The core of this book is a template for strategic planning and creating a strategic plan. We go through all the elements to include in a comprehensive strategic plan.

The strategic plan is the crucial link between strategic thinking and action or strategic implementation.

The plan is the course you have set to reach your destination goal. Seneca said, "if one does not know to which port one is sailing, no wind is favorable."

You have to know where you are going or you won't end up there.

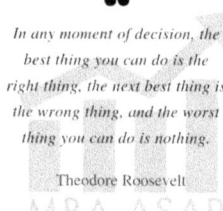

In any moment of decision, the best thing you can do is the right thing, the next best thing is the wrong thing, and the worst thing you can do is nothing.

Theodore Roosevelt

The less you control what you do, the more what you do controls you. The strategic plan puts you in control of what you do.

1
INTRODUCTION TO BUSINESS STRATEGY

Strategy in business is the big picture. Planning and implementing a strategic vision is how a business succeeds and is profitable.

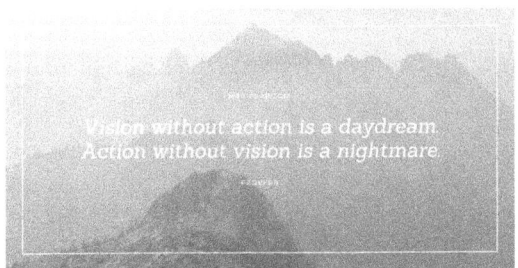

STRATEGY IS about figuring out how to create a sustainable competitive advantage and barriers to entering your markets. Strategy is a firm's answer to the following question: What can we do that is really hard?

. . .

GREAT STRATEGY LOCATES and exploits the fit between market conditions and a firm's assets.

> "It had long since come to my attention that people of accomplishment rarely sat back and let things happen to them. They went out and happened to things."
>
> **Leonardo da Vinci**

LEADERSHIP AND MANAGEMENT are the key skill sets that rely on strategy. Leadership is doing the right things. Management is doing things right.

STRATEGIC THINKING and vision is the realm of leadership.

STRATEGIC IMPLEMENTATION and executing the strategy is the realm of management.

STRATEGIC PLANNING BRINGS the skills of leadership and management together.

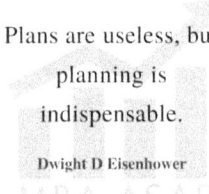

> Plans are useless, but planning is indispensable.
>
> Dwight D Eisenhower

BUSINESS STRATEGY IS about picking goals for the enterprise and then figuring out what resources are going to be assembled to achieve those goals.

2
THE IMPORTANCE OF A STRATEGIC MINDSET

"To think is easy. To act is hard. But the hardest thing in the world is to act in accordance with your thinking."
— Johann Wolfgang von Goethe

The importance of strategy is to provide a framework so we can act in accordance with our thinking. It provides a set of tools and techniques to help us achieve those hard things.

A FOX KNOWS MANY THINGS, but a hedgehog one important thing. Both approaches are valid and we should examine ourselves and pick the one the suits our personality. A strategic mindset makes things happen. Turn dreams into reality and get things done.

Prevent Piss Poor Performance with Planning

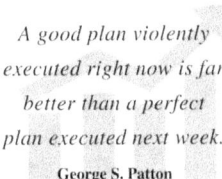

> *A good plan violently executed right now is far better than a perfect plan executed next week.*
> — George S. Patton

JACK HANDEY SAID:

"It's easy to sit there and say you'd like to have more money.

And I guess that's what I like about it.

It's easy.

Just sitting there, rocking back and forth, wanting that money."

JACK HANDEY IS hilarious and his point is well taken. It's easy to think about stuff without taking any action to make it happen.

A GOAL without a plan is just a wish.

A PLAN without action is a dream and action without a plan is a nightmare.

> *Between the idea*
> *And the reality*
> *Between the motion*
> *And the act*
> *Falls the Shadow*
> T.S. Eliot, The Hollow Men

To act is to implement solutions.

Hard work pays off. Without hard work, a great strategy remains a dream.

Is your ladder against the right wall? Without a great strategy, hard work becomes a nightmare.

Strategic Thinking, Planning, and Implementation all work together. Results only occur when all three steps are working in concert.

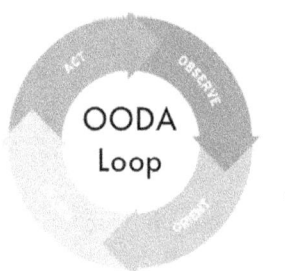

OODA loop refers to the decision cycle of observe, orient, decide, and act, developed by military strategist and United States Air Force Colonel John Boyd.

3
STRATEGIC PLANNING

Proper Planning and Preparation Prevents Painfully Poor Performance

The 7 Ps is a British Army adage for Proper Planning and Preparation Prevents Piss Poor Performance. Cheeky Brits. But the meaning is crucial. Planning is an essential part of launching and growing a successful business.

STRATEGIC PLANNING UNCOVERS critical issues driving a business. These issues can be problems, opportunities, market changes, resource adjustments, and anything else that requires a solution or decision.

IF YOU FAIL TO PLAN, you plan to fail.

. . .

Having a strategy and a practical plan for carrying it out doesn't just apply to business. It is a critical part of leading a successful life. As Ryan Holiday has said,

> The hard things in life are not achieved through simple effort and energy. If they were, a lot of people would do them. It's insight that illuminates the path. It's strategy that gets us there.

As part of the strategic planning process, question everything. Challenge all the assumptions upon which the past strategic initiatives have been based. And examine strategic implementation:

- What needs to be addressed?
- What are we doing now that we shouldn't be doing?
- What should we do differently?
- Is there a better way to do something?

These are some of the types of questions that strategic leaders ask to jump-start the process.

> A good plan is like a road map: it shows the final destination and usually the best way to get there.
> H. Stanley Judd

A strategic plan is a roadmap to launch and grow your business. It's your map of how to do more with less. Remember, a map is not the territory, and your plan is not a static document but subject to continuous revision as you confront events and the world.

BY THEIR NATURE, all plans and maps are reduced and abstract, and by doing so, eliminate information that can prove vital. The most accurate plan would include everything.

> The best material model of a cat is another, or preferably the same, cat.
> Norbert Wiener

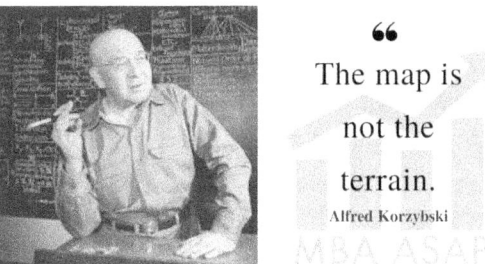

> "The map is not the terrain.
> Alfred Korzybski

THIS PARTIAL INFORMATION, coupled with uncertainty about future events, means a plan is not a perfect document to act upon and must be open to revision as new information becomes available.

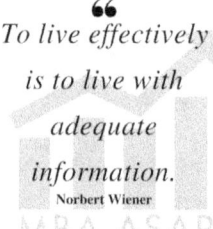

> *To live effectively is to live with adequate information.*
> Norbert Wiener

AS THE GREAT Prussian military genius Field Marshall Von Moltke said:

"No battle plan survives contact with the enemy."

A strategic plan is not a blueprint but merely a set of guesses to be tested in the marketplace. Most plans are hallucinations. No plan survives contact with customers and competitors intact.

4

PLANS ARE USELESS; PLANNING IS INVALUABLE

> In preparing for battle, I have always found that plans are useless, but planning is indispensable.
> - Dwight D. Eisenhower

The reason for the military references is that strategic thinking and planning came out of a military background and was appropriated by the business world.

WHEN IT COMES to strategic planning, the process is more important than the product. It's not the plan document, but the planning process that is valuable and also your ability to course correct in the face of new information. It is essential to remain flexible and adaptive and have contingency plans to address various possible futures.

THINK of strategic planning as having four main interlocking and iterative stages:

- Analysis and Assessment
- Strategy Development
- Strategy Execution
- Evaluation and Refinement

This outline provides a context for thinking about the strategic plan, not as a fixed static document, but as part of an ongoing organic process.

THE STRATEGIC PLANNING process and plan address what we are trying to fix, accomplish, or avoid. Communicating your strategy aligns stakeholders around your priorities. It engages, motivates, and retains both internal and external audiences.

THE GOAL IS to answer the question: how will we succeed? Strategies are the methods you intend to implement to achieve your vision. Strategy determines what you want to achieve and why, and most important, it answers the question "how." The strategic plan aligns your mission, programs, and capacity.

5
ELEMENTS TO INCLUDE IN YOUR STRATEGIC PLAN

The information below outlines the key elements to cover in your plan.

Table of Contents

Here is an outline. Your table of contents should look something like below. Feel free to change the order, so the flow fits your thinking.

Here is a detailed look at each element.

Executive Summary

The Executive Summary should be first in the document but completed last. As the name says, it summarizes the other sections of your plan, so you need to spend the time crafting the other parts first.

THE EXECUTIVE SUMMARY IS CRITICAL. Keep it to one page. It should succinctly convey the future direction, priorities, and their impact. It's about vision and execution. You want to be doing the right things and creating a roadmap for doing things right.

THE DISCIPLINE OF CREATING A CONCISE, crisp distillation of your strategy is well worth the effort. Many of your key constituents will only read the summary, and you want them to understand where you intend to go and be engaged in the execution.

WHEN HARRY TRUMAN suddenly became president after the death of FDR, General Leslie Groves met with him to brief him on the Manhattan Project. Groves brought volumes of material to leave with the new president. Truman ordered Groves to come back with a one-page summary. Groves said he couldn't possibly reduce such a complicated program to a single page. Truman told him that he didn't understand the program until he could put it on one page. Groves then went and did it. Truman's exhortation is excellent advice to all of us. Keep it in mind as you write your summary.

Elevator Pitch

An elevator pitch is a brief description of your business. It got its name as the challenge of having a story about your business prepared that you can deliver in the course of an elevator ride. Include it early in your strategic plan because it distills what is essential and unique about your business.

. . .

THE CLARITY of your elevator pitch is key to your business' success. Customers and investors need to understand it. It impacts your ability to recruit and retain top talent. Everyone in the organization needs to be able to clearly and concisely articulate the business.

Mission, Vision, and Values

Here is where you state your purpose and why what you are doing represents meaningful work.

Mission Statement

The Mission Statement Answers the following:

- What is our purpose?
- Why do we exist?
- What do we do?

Your mission statement explains what your business is trying to achieve. It provides the criteria that guide managers' and employees' decisions that align with the company's goals.

YOUR MISSION STATEMENT is what defines the guardrails of what your business is and isn't. It explains why what the company is doing represents meaningful work. Contributing to meaningful work is what motivates employees.

. . .

IT IS ALSO the main message delivered to external stakeholders, such as investors, partners, potential employees, and customers. It should inspire them to take the actions you want.

Vision Statement

> You cannot change your destination overnight, but you can change your direction overnight.
> - Jim Rohn

Every project starts as a vision in the imagination. A Vision Statement defines that desired future state and provides direction for an organization.

THE VISION STATEMENT addresses the question: where are we going? And as Yogi Berra said,

> "If you don't know where you are going, you might wind up someplace else."

It is critical to articulate a vision that inspires all the stakeholders to agree. It is fruitless to expect people to act upon strategies and tactics enthusiastically if they don't believe in the ultimate goals and vision.

THE BULK of the strategic plan is devoted to addressing how we will get there.

Priorities

This general heading includes objectives, goals, and action items and how you are going to measure them. This section attempts to balance the aspirational and forward-looking with the specific and tangible.

Objectives

> The greater danger for most of us isn't that our aim is too high and we miss it, but that it is too low and we reach it.
> - Michaelangelo

Articulating objectives is where we set priorities. What are the major things we must focus on to reach our vision? What are the "big rocks" that we need to put in place first and foremost?

IDENTIFY key objectives for all areas of your organization, including financial, customer, marketing, operations, and human resources.

Goals

> A goal is a dream with a deadline.
> - Napoleon Hill

Goals express a result. Goals allow us to focus on the most important actions to reach our strategic objectives.

Goals can be formatted using the SMART template: Specific, Measurable, Attainable, Realistic, and Time-bound.

> A goal properly set is halfway reached.
> - Zig Ziglar

Strategic planning is all about setting and achieving goals. The ability to execute is the hallmark of successful companies.

IDENTIFY YOUR LONG-TERM GOALS. Then, identify interim milestone goals that you must achieve to maintain the pace and path to achieving your long-term goals.

WORK BACKWARD to create more granular goals for the next months and quarters. Boeing is legendary for the granularity of their planning. They break five-year plans into day-by-day goals and milestones.

WHEN IT COMES TO IMPLEMENTATION, take care of the short-term and the long-term will take care of itself. There are no long-term results without short-term results.

REVISIT YOUR PLAN REGULARLY, update your progress, and revise as necessary. A strategy is an iterative process.

Action Items

You plan your work, and then you work your plan.

DECISIVE ACTION IS how you make a strategy work. Action items are assigned and accountable tactics. Who will do what by when?

THESE ARE functional items that align with, and support, the accomplishment of the objectives and goals.

> "Plans are only good intentions unless they immediately degenerate into hard work."
> - Peter Drucker

ACTION ITEMS IDENTIFY legitimate work to be done. The only legitimate work in an organization is work that moves the mission forward.

Measurement

> "What gets measured, gets managed."
> Peter Drucker

How will we measure success? **OKRs** and **KPIs** are ways to organize measuring performance.

Objectives and Key Results (OKRs)

Objectives and key results is a framework for defining and tracking objectives and their outcomes. Major Silicon Valley companies, including Google, LinkedIn, Twitter, and Uber, use this framework. The legendary venture capitalist John Doerr has written an excellent book on OKRs called Measure What Matters. He names Andy Grove of Intel fame, the "Father of OKRs."

Key Performance Indicators (KPIs)

KPIs are the metrics that will have the most impact on moving your organization forward. Measuring the KPIs, and acting upon the feedback, are how you course correct. Guide your organization with measures that matter.

TRACKING YOUR KPIS.

Businesses leaders intimately understand and are obsessive in measuring their metrics and KPIs. Tracking is how you know how your business is performing so you can adjust as needed.

A PRIMARY KPI such as Total Sales is critical for understanding if the company is performing well. Understanding and measuring the drivers of sales is also essential so you can anticipate and address issues quickly. KPIs help a company be responsive to changes in the environment in which they operate.

. . .

LIST THE KPIs you will track in your business.

Marketing Plan

How do your strategic initiatives impact and enhance your brand?

YOUR MARKETING PLAN describes who your customer segments are and how you will move them through your sales funnel. It talks about customer acquisition costs (CAC) and maximizing lifetime value (LTV). Remember CAC<LTV.

INCLUDE a detailed summary of your marketing plan in your strategic plan. Emphasize and prioritize critical elements.

Target Customers

This section of your strategic plan is for identifying your target customer clusters. Use marketing templates like **STP: Segmentation, Targeting, and Positioning** to help organize this planning.

IT'S essential to focus your marketing efforts to be effective and efficient in reaching and addressing potential customers. Hone your messaging and ensure it speaks to your target customer wants and needs.

Environmental Analysis

Environmental analysis is where you analyze your organization's position in the broader context of outside influences and competitors. You can use PEST and SWOT formats for clearly organizing this information.

PEST

PEST stands for political, economic, social, technological factors that affect your organization's mission and approach.

SWOT

SWOT is a template that stands for Strengths, Weaknesses, Opportunities, and Threats. A SWOT analysis examines an organization's internal strengths and weaknesses with external opportunities and threats.

SWOT IS a quick way to assess and describe your competitive position.

ITS IMPORTANCE in the Strategic Plan is to rank and determine the best opportunities to pursue relative to achieving your goals.

USE it to identify which strengths and core competencies to allocate resources to improve your company's competitive position.

SOWT Analysis

My friend Brenner Adams, a brilliant marketer and strategist, didn't think SWOT was stacked right. So he came up with So What: SWOT.

SOWT IS MORE than an arbitrary list of strengths, weaknesses, threats, and opportunities; it's a formula for action. In a SOWT analysis, strengths align with opportunities, and weaknesses align with threats horizontally. Matching strengths to a market or consumer opportunity, for example, leads to insights, which drive quicker and more effective decision-making.

WEAKNESSES AND THREATS are evaluated the same way: a company will list out the weaknesses they determine internally based on the market, the product, or the team. Then, they can compare that list to one of the threats faced, whether from competing products or market risks, and leverage the resulting insight to prioritize the challenges to draw actionable conclusions and build plans to mitigate those external factors.

ONCE YOU ALIGN your strengths and your opportunities, you can get insights. Weakness and strengths determine what actions you need to take to prevent getting surprised and ambushed. You're not going to have every answer, but you become aware of what some of the blind spots could be.

. . .

SOWT drives initial strategic prioritization and thinking.

Industry Analysis

You want to understand your industry and ensure your addressable market size is expanding. If it is not, consider diversification. Analyzing the structure and dynamics of your industry will help uncover new opportunities for growth.

Competitive Analysis & Advantage

What do we do best? What are our core competencies?

What characteristics of our organization enable us to meet our customer's needs better than our competition can? What are we best at in our market and the eyes of our customers?

Identify your key competitors and substitute products and do a SWOT analysis on each one.

Use this analysis to determine your competitive advantages and strategies to enhance and strengthen them.

Human Resources

Do you have the capacity and competencies to achieve your goals? Identify the skill sets needed to execute on the opportunities you've identified and to achieve the goals you have established. Do you have the human resources required to execute your plan?

LIST your current team members and identify the skill sets you need to hire to achieve your goals. Include a timeline for on-boarding.

Operations Plan

Operations are what transform your goals and opportunities into reality. Identify the individual projects that comprise your larger goals and how to execute these projects. Use project management tools Gantt and PERT charts to detail each initiative. Know when each project will start, what the budgets are, what the critical paths are, and who will lead them, and be responsible for execution and completion.

Financial Projections

The financial projections need to align with your aspirations. The pro forma financials is where each element is quantified, budgets created, and timelines established.

USE a financial model spreadsheet and NPV and IRR to assess the possible results for each opportunity you consider pursuing. These are your decision-making tools.

. . .

THE FINANCIAL PROJECTIONS map out the tactics in detail. The projections are the road map to implementation and execution.

6
SUMMARY

Now you are ready to write your Executive Summary.
Review and revise your strategic plan during an annual planning session solely dedicated to focusing on this work. Update it regularly as you gather results, and gain more clarity.

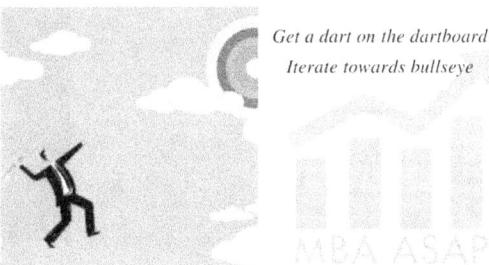

Get a dart on the dartboard
Iterate towards bullseye

YOU WILL NOT ACHIEVE the precise goals established in your strategic plan. The art is in making those goals aggressive but achievable. Research shows that you'll come much closer to them versus if you didn't plan at all. It's not about the plan; it's about the planning.

> Plans are only good intentions unless they immediately degenerate into hard work.
> - Peter Drucker

The world will push back against your strategic plan.

Be fluid and prepared to course correct as you encounter obstacles.

> No battle plan survives contact with the enemy.
> Helmuth von Moltke

> It is not the strongest of the species that survives, nor the most intelligent; it is the one most adaptable to change.
> Charles Darwin

Persist in Your Efforts.

Fail until you don't.

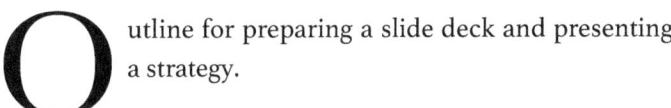

PRESENT YOUR STRATEGY IN A HANDFUL OF SLIDES

Six Slides Needed to Present a Strategy

Outline for preparing a slide deck and presenting a strategy.

THE ABILITY TO communicate your strategic thinking is what defines a leader. When you create a strategy, it is an opportunity to prove that you are a leader.

A WELL-DESIGNED presentation is one of the best ways to communicate your strategic thinking. It is a critical part of a strategy sequence — research, analyze, build strategy, present strategy, execute strategy, report back on results.

YOU CAN DELIVER an excellent strategy presentation in as little as six slides.

A strategy is not a plan.

A list of executable tactics with a timeline attached is a plan. A strategy is more than that. A strategy is how you convince stakeholders that your project is excellent and achieve buy-in.

THE TACTICS ARE THE "WHAT." The goal is the "why." The strategy is the "how." It's the guiding principle.

YOU CAN HAVE a plan full of tactics but lacking strategy, and it will fall flat with stakeholders. Present the same list of tactics, but preface that with a solid strategy, and you'll get the approval you're seeking.

A strategy is not a spreadsheet.

A strategy develops and evolves in brainstorming sessions after research and data gathering. The strategic thinking may come together on a whiteboard or in a spreadsheet. The best way to present your strategy is in the form of a slide deck using PowerPoint or an equivalent presentation program.

PRESENTING IS STORYTELLING. You want to engage your audience. Slides are excellent for storytelling because you can control your narrative's direction and pace and emphasize emotion through visual design.

. . .

START by presenting slides and use spreadsheet data for support.

You only need six slides.

There are many ways to build a strategy, but certain elements lead to a well-received strategy presentation. Here is an outline of the essential slides.

1. Task at Hand
2. Insight
3. Principles
4. Visual Model
5. Tactics
6. Timing

Slide 1 — Task at Hand

Make your first slide a clear and concise description of the job to be done. Include the specific goal or business problem.

IT COULD BE A WELL-WRITTEN sentence or two; it could be a graph or a single number; it could be an image that instantly illustrates the problem to your audience. It's likely some combination of these.

AIM FOR IMPACT through brevity on your first slide. What you say during this slide doesn't need to be written on it.

You can elaborate verbally to provide context. Try not to let your audience read the slide. You don't want your audience reading; you want them focused on what you are saying.

Slide 2 — Insight

If you're at the point where you're creating slides, then you've already spent some time researching and collecting data.

AN INSIGHT IS an observation plus understanding. It's research and data plus a storyline that knits it together.

THE INSIGHT SLIDE of your presentation contains sentences. Keep your data and findings in the appendix and pull them up if asked.

Slide 3: Principles

Slide 3 is the first slide that gets into your strategy. You have expressed the problem and the insights into it; it's time to show how you will solve the issue.

> *Vision without execution is just hallucination.*
> Thomas Edison

THIS SLIDE NEEDS to be impactful. Make it clear and concise and use sticky language.

BY "STICKY," I mean you want your audience to be able to instantly recall and carry this slide's idea with them after your presentation. Word choice matters here. The slide layout, your pace, and tone of voice all matter and impact your ability to make it memorable.

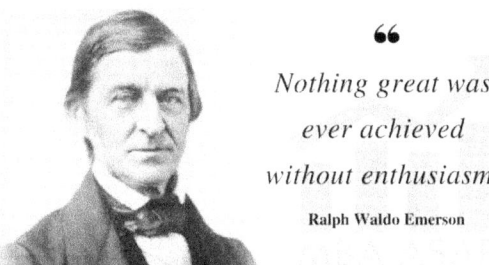

HOOK YOUR AUDIENCE. Get everybody excited about your approach. Lead with impact and follow with detail.

Slide 4: Visual Model

A strategy proposes that the desired outcome is achievable if you approach a problem in the proposed way. It's a prediction of what could become a reality, based on data, experience, insights, and creativity. A visual model facilitates understanding.

. . .

Your visual model should show the inputs, steps, or actions and their priority or sequence. Illustrate the process or system that will deliver the desired outcome.

Some model format examples are:

- 4-quadrant
- Three pillars
- Funnel
- Pyramid
- Venn diagram
- Flywheel

Google these terms for examples and inspiration.

The visual model can be one of the best ways to ensure understanding and acceptance of your strategy. Think it through carefully and get feedback from peers before your presentation.

Slide 5: Tactics

This next section is where you include the details. Describe the exact steps or tactics in your plan. The format can be straightforward. Your writing should be clear and concise.

. . .

THIS PART of your presentation might be more than one slide. Keep in mind that less is more.

AS YOU WORK on this section, ask yourself what questions might come up. If the answers are easy, incorporate them into the presentation. If the answers are tangential, put them in an appendix and avoid a distracting tangent if the question never comes up.

Slide 6: Timing

> A goal is a dream with a deadline.
> - Napoleon Hill

DETAIL the anticipated length of each phase of your strategic implementation in days, weeks, or months. Are there any key milestones and deliverables you plan to hit?

COMMIT to communicating and presenting progress or results back to the key stakeholders. Don't wait to notify interested parties of any unanticipated obstacles you encounter, and don't try to sugarcoat delays or cost over-runs. Keep everyone in the loop.

WHAT IS the date you expect to have achieved the goal? Set realistic expectations. Then try to do it all sooner; under-promise and over-deliver.

> *Well done is better than well said.*
> Benjamin Franklin

Slide 7 — Conclusion.

An impactful strategy presentation takes just six essential slides. But you might want to wrap up the presentation with a summary slide.

SUMMARIZE with a list of immediate next steps, or wrap it up with a motivational quote. Or a slide with the word "questions?" to indicate that it's time for discussion and feedback.

Two more things guarantee a productive presentation.

Send out a pre-read of the slides before your presentation. This step will help keep the meeting on track. Primed and prepared participants elevate the quality of questions and discussion.

PRACTICE PRESENTING your strategy without notes. You wrote the slides — you know what's on them, you don't need a script. Internalize the story and tell it with enthusiasm and conviction.

. . .

Record a run-through on your phone and review it. Do this a few times, and you will have a polished delivery.

Next time you get asked what your strategy is, you'll know exactly how to tell the story and sell your strategic vision.

The End

Plans are only good intentions **unless** they immediately degenerate into hard **work**.
 - Peter Drucker

Now get to work.

Thank you for reading!

I hope you enjoyed **Prevent Piss Poor Performance with Planning** and found it filled with useful and valuable information..

As an author, I love feedback. Candidly, you are the reason that I organize my thoughts, write, and explore these topics. So, tell me what you liked, what was helpful and what could be better explained or left out. You can write me at jjcousins@gmail.com and visit me on the web at www.mba-asap.com.

Finally, I need to ask a favor. If you're so inclined, I'd love a review on Amazon of **Prevent Piss Poor Performance with Planning**. I'd really appreciate your feedback.

Reviews can be tough to come by these days. You, the reader, have the power now to make or break a book. If you have the time, here's a link to my author page on Amazon where you can find all of my books: https://www.amazon.com/-/e/B01JVF2XTU or just search for the title and my name on Amazon. A quick review will be immensely appreciated!

Thank you so much for reading and for spending the time and effort with me.

In deep gratitude,
JOHN COUSINS

RECEIVE ANNOUNCEMENTS OF FREE AND DISCOUNTED BOOKS AND COURSES.

Sign up for my Newsletter and get free books and special offers. Sign up at **www.mba-asap.com** and **receive Reading and Understanding Financial Statements absolutely free.**

ABOUT THE AUTHOR

John is an author, blogger, podcaster, online course creator, investor, inventor, entrepreneur and musician. John began his career, after graduating from Boston University and MIT with degrees in Media Studies and Electronics, working for one of the great early Silicon Valley tech firms: Ampex. He then spent a decade in Manhattan working for ABC Television as a systems engineer designing and building facilities for the network and managing programs for sports and news; big spectacles like the Olympics and political conventions.

John then received his MBA from Wharton. He has since taken two companies public as CFO and CEO and has had 15 years experience as a public company CFO and ten years experience as a public company CEO. John has been involved in many start up and public company financings and deal making. He has founded numerous startups in alternative energy, life sciences, and technology. His career shifted to teaching at numerous universities in US and internationally in the past ten years. His company MBA ASAP delivers digital content on business topics via eBooks, paperbacks, audiobooks, podcasts and online courses. Visit http://www.mba-asap.com/

ALSO BY JOHN COUSINS

MBA ASAP: Master the Game of Business

Understanding Corporate Finance: MBA ASAP

MBA ASAP Marketing 2.0: Principles and Practice in the Digital Age

www.ingramcontent.com/pod-product-compliance
Lightning Source LLC
Chambersburg PA
CBHW070855220526
45466CB00005B/2009